avalon

in a different light

contents

Photography by Matt Barnes

ISBN 0-634-00590-1

HAL•LEONARD®
CORPORATION
7777 W. BLUEMOUND RD. P.O. BOX 13819 MILWAUKEE, WI 53213

Visit Hal Leonard Online at
www.halleonard.com

always have, always will

Words and Music by GRANT CUNNINGHAM,
TOBY McKEEHAN and NICK GONZALES

Part of me __ is the pro - di - gal, part of me __ is the oth - er broth - er.
I was born __ with a way - ward heart; still I live __ with the rest - less spir - it.

(Harmony 2nd time only)

3

take you at your word

Words and Music by PAUL FIELD
and GRANT CUNNINGHAM

Oh. _____ Oh. _____

Lord, I love_ You, oh, ___ and I trust_ You. As ___ I live I've learned _

___ I ___ can take You at Your word._

Your ___ Your word _ is love. Your word_

first love

Words and Music by HENK POOL,
SAM SCOTT and LEE ANN VERMEULEN

MCA Music Publishing

Male: Fa - ther, take ___ me back, ___ let me start _____ a - gain. ___ Lord, I've failed and I've fall - en in ___ my pride. _____

Back _____ to You. _____

Lead me back _____ to You, _____

With pedal

can't live a day

Words and Music by CONNIE HARRINGTON,
JOE BECK and TY LACY

Slowly

I could live life a lone ___ and nev-er fill ___ the long-
could trav-el the world, ___ see all the won-ders beau-

-ings of ___ my heart, ___ the heal-ing warmth ___ of some-one's ___ arms. And I ___
-ti-ful ___ and new. ___ They'd on-ly make ___ me think ___ of ___ You. And I ___

(Harmony 2nd time only)

could live with-out ___ dreams, ___ and nev-er know ___ the thrill ___
could have all life ___ of-fered, ___ rich-es that ___ were far ___

i'm speechless

Words and Music by TY LACY
and JOANNA CARLSON

hide my soul

Written by CHRIS EATON
and SHEILA WALSH

D.S. al Coda

do do do doot doot do do do do, do do do doot doot do do do do.

___ and there ___ will ___ be ___ no ___ pain ___ in ___ heav-en. _

Do do do doot doot do do do do

do do do doot doot do do do do. ___

in a different light

Words and Music by JODY McBRAYER, CHERIE PALIOTTA,
MICHAEL PASSONS, JANNA POTTER and MATT HUESMANN

Don't cry for me. ___
Don't be a - fraid ___

No, I've ___ nev - er been ___ one to shoul - der the weight ___ of the world.
of the twists and the turns of the road ___ that we're on. ___ Just be - lieve ___

in not of

Words and Music by GRANT CUNNINGHAM
and NICK GONZALES

let your love

Words and Music by JEFF BORDERS,
PHIL MADEIRA and GAYLA BORDERS

I can hear You call - ing; _____ in a
been un - chang - ing. _____ I have

whis - per _____ You say so _____ much. _____ In a
seen my _____ world spin - ning _____ by. _____ On - ly

only for the weak

Words and Music by SCOTT KRIPPAYNE,
MICHAEL PURYEAR and DOAK SNEAD

*Vocals written one octave higher than sung.

if my people pray

Words and Music by DOUG McKELVEY,
MATT HUESMANN and KENT HOOPER